alvin greenberg
the house of the would-be gardener

alvin greenberg

the house
of the
would-be gardener

with drawings by
john tuska

new rivers press / new york 1972

most of these poems have appeared in the following publica-
tions and permission to reprint is gratefully acknowledged:

antioch review
epoch
gnosis
hanging loose
hiram poetry review
the little magazine
new: american and canadian poetry

northstone review
ohio review
perspective
poetry northwest
quartet
yes

DISTRIBUTION:

in great britain:

    philip spender
    69 randolph avenue
    london, w9, england

in the u.s. and elsewhere:

    serendipity books
    1790 shattuck avenue
    berkeley, california
    94709

this book was manufactured in the united states of america for
new rivers press, p.o. box 578, cathedral station, new york, n.y.
10025 in a first edition of 750 copies of which 500 have been
bound in paper and 250 in cloth with 30 of the cloth edition
signed and numbered by the author

OTHER BOOKS BY ALVIN GREENBERG

THE SMALL WAVES (el corno emplumado—1965) — novel
THE METAPHYSICAL GIRAFFE (new rivers—1968) — poems
GOING NOWHERE (simon and schuster-1971) — novel

for marsha

contents

i.   the preservation of the self in everyday life

dream one

the number of lives in my life
is exceedingly many, and the colors

that glow in their fur
not to be lost sight of in the twilight,

and the days of the week of their comings
and goings remembered,

and promises made to them and
promises they have promised to keep

and the particular song that each one sings
from the long catalogue of their music

in my head.

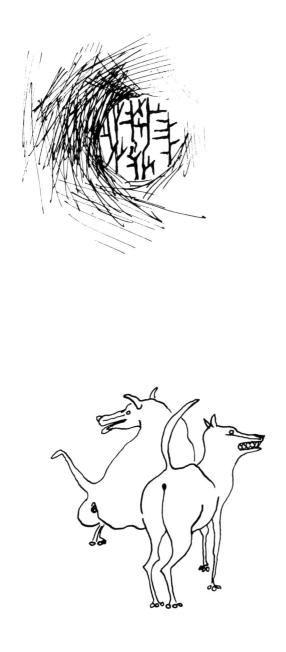

Tusha 1972

dream two

we live in an age of inflation:
the older we get,
the higher the price of skin and bones;

the higher the price of skin and bones,
the more we risk
each day we tumble among these mountains;

the more we risk,
the sooner we meet
the twilight animals
at play in the valleys of our bones: there

bears cash in their furs and plunge
and we, too, turn upon the peaks
and plunge.

refrain

we all have black shadows:

i wrap myself up in mine
and disappear.

dream three: help from the gods

i need:

a dog as big as the moon
and stupid enough to challenge the gates of hell.

they say:

'your wish is granted:
                    good luck

at the other end of the leash.'

dream four

more snow than anyone has ever seen before:

snow drifting against the top storeys
of all the office buildings

snow filling in the whole mississippi valley

and i keep saying, 'i'm not
cold, i'm not cold' and let myself go drifting

deep into the valley between your breasts.

allegory

a long narrative poem
in which everyone aspires

(and some, to a degree, even manage)

to become roger.

dream five

my guide to proper diet says
'all animals are merely converted vegetables.'

we poll the chickens on that,
the haddock and the wombats
and those who are closest to the ground of all,

the children

who salt and pepper one another in the park
and announce:
                'this

is the delight you've been preparing us for all along.'

i look around behind the swings and teeter-totters
for that shadowy refrain to curl up into.

dream six: polonaise

i am carving the sunday roast.
each delicate slice curls from my knife

and slips into the pool of blood
in the center of the platter.

i have plenty of time to spear each one

with a fork, in the midst of its descent,
and decree: stay dry!

but i am busy.
                    I am slicing
the red roast,
                    slicing
the meat,
            slicing
busily,
            slicing

        slicing

    slicing

cing

dream seven

the insufferable miner
has muscled in on all his friends' claims.

'there's nothing here,' they tell him,
'just an old moraine.
our camps are only fit for building sites.'

but he brushes aside the snow without a word
and rams his pickaxe into the frozen ground
and then goes off and leaves it sticking there
and his friends with the job of prying it loose.

one by one they all turn to it

leaning against it the weight of lives
with chunks of rock locked up in them

like fossils.

the unexpected

the neanderthal of my own past
hunkers down with a bone in his hand
in the shadow of a rock whose exact location
only i know.

he waits to see if i dare to pass that way.

dream eight

rivers that shift about in the spring
like small boys. old men
who re-dream the french revolution every night.

the structure of november, in which,
for a moment, all things hold still:

rivers drop to their knees
and the day-to-day firing stops

and we are walking on an island of oaks
where two rivers meet in floodtime
to deposit a mountain of agates.

out of this, a single stone,
shaded like a rainbow,

that i can carry home through any streets.

commentary

when this building settles
and cracks begin to appear in its walls

then

it'll be real enough to live in.

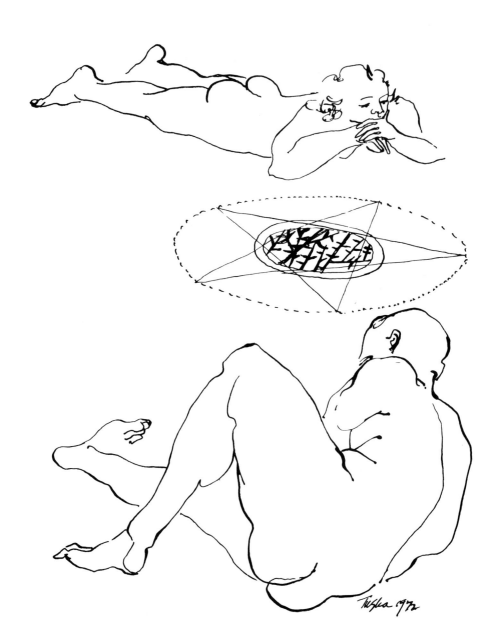

dream nine

the neighbors have hung out shingles
to identify their professions

but i can't even read them.

they are committed to significant strategies,
according to the seasons,
in their garages and backyards

but it's all i can do to keep mine clean.

they converge in lumbering trajectories
on a spot marked x

that i can't bring myself to step aside from

seeing how at the distance of a few feet
they explode softly

and the air around me lights up with real people.

dream ten: moving in

already pencil-thin lines finger the walls
in corners, up near the ceiling.

'you said it would be perfect,' you say,
as i had asked you to do when the moment came,

but i forget what my answer was supposed to be.
what i say instead is:

'even the shadows are real and have
real shadows too'

for a thin red trickle
has begun to seep from every crack.

by the time we return with our belongings
spiders are already at work in the corners,
knitting up the damage.

for the first time,
i hate them with a clear conscience.

conservation

even the golden eagle,
who can outfly me any day of the week,
has protection under federal law

though there are fewer of me than him.

dream eleven

here, in an immense twilight
perpetrated by all my physical complaints,

out of which those of good humor among us
try to devise simply

'another winter'

is the irritable point where three roads cross:
the self in time.
i try to keep my footing on the icy sidewalks

but the crowd i travel in has no mercy.
x-rays peddle unacceptable rumors about my lungs
and i am given no chance to deny anything.

my bones tell tales on the essential me.

dream twelve

voices that sang barroom songs and brayed
and voices chanting over small objects at dawn
voices that spilled out into the rain

voices that cradled the snow
voices that lay dry and cracking in the streets

a pair of voices saying yes and no, yes and no

voices that spoke of other things, other things
a voice that failed to become a voice at all

a voice that could speak in no
other voices than its own and one
that could only speak in other voices

a voice where there were no listeners, none
and the last voice of all, saying go forth

and do as little damage as possible.

dream thirteen

months pass, and just when
the air all around me grows bald
and frost nips the hairs

on the theme of transportation
and even the dog reveals a preference
for walking himself,

i wander into an experience with fur:

a soft fuzz
that springs up wherever my hands travel

saying, in each place, 'this
is where i am, and this
i, and this

still another i, and

look . . . there now . . .
growing from the tips of your own fingers . . . '

message

in that same sky
full of raindrops and falling bodies
there is also an airplane en route to vienna

picking its way through the clutter of the present tense
(i go, i fly, i touch, i sing, i love)

with an announcement,
to a friend.

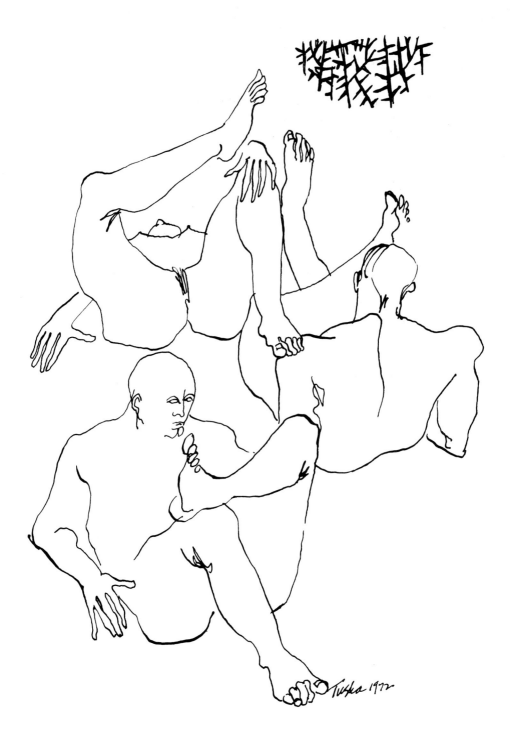

dream fourteen

on a scruffy beach at lake huron or in new
york city or in a library
in argentina

one's own characters brush their teeth and gargle
and put on their literary outfits

and begin to clamber down the beanstalk
toward home:

they emerge from the clouds rump first
and the whole apparatus sways in the sky
and leaves torn in their passing
precede them

and the axe is dull and the neighbors hilarious

and there's nothing to do but sit down
in the shade of their arrival and say, 'i

did this? i
did this?'

dream fifteen

the invention of this machine
solves everything:

the sky turns blue
the instant it's set in motion.
pickles taste better.

family men know the value of this thing
and place their wives and children

in rhythm with it.
when it visits the suburbs
it passes approval on each backyard

and then hovers above it, waiting for applause.

at ours, it waits and waits.
days pass and tassels grow shaggy on the corn
before it realizes

we are waiting up there beside it.

little song

bone on shadowy bone goes
crack: this dark eclipse of music

has ears and fur itself, and's
what i've made to travel with.

dream sixteen

rainbow colored moss flows up the wall,
forcing vowel changes

out of each word inscribed on each brick:
'moan' to 'moon', 'bane' to 'bone'

'soon' to 'now'—
and then at the top squeezes up

names of flowers that are also names of people.

through that lush foliage i scramble over
and drop to the grass on the other side,

an agile escapee carrying your name,

a russian name,
bent in the russian style and imbedded
in my own flesh,

doing the work of many ligaments.

dream seventeen

we enter another world now,
in which time moves less quickly:

where the trajectory of a bullet
is a dotted line whose end we can all see
and step aside from,

where the moment of our waking together
goes on and on

and we live recklessly inside it.

envoi

in this land i am the native *and*
the anthropologist.

between us on the dirt floor
burns a small fire, called

'the "rightness" of my own ceremonies.'

ii.   bone flights

Tusha 1972

directions

the sun is so far south
that even at noon the trees send long shadows north,
telling us to go that way also.

you did.   i followed after:
a dizzying journey.   the world
spins us and spins us
and then sends us its
way,
pin in hand.

when the blindfold is removed
we blink and find ourselves facing each other
in a territory neither of us knew was there.

clumsy with care
we set about using those dull pins
to open a network of paths.

then we flow along them,
making this world ours too.

the original flying poem

1. the news of my sudden passing
   fills the airport with these
   relatives. they're all there,
   excepting one distant cousin

2. in tanganyika. i greet them in
   dark suit and chauffeur's cap.

3. 'the best-loved of your family
   is gone,' i inform them as we
   drive, 'note, meanwhile, that
   we're crossing the mississippi.'

4. a cousin lovely and less than
   distant sniffles beside me in
   the front seat. 'there will be
   no funeral,' i whisper to her
   alone. her reply is more tears.

5. it takes many trips. such an
   expansive family! and so many
   crossings and recrossings of
   the mississippi. i apologize
   for the colorless bluffs: 'it's
   been a very disappointing fall.'

6. at last they have all gone inside. they have chairs and food,
   and i am in this vehicle alone,

7. wondering how to reimburse them
   for the expenses of such travel.

a new astronomy

it was the night to have brought
the beginning of spring—if there

had been springs in such a tropic.
from the roof we saw clouds flee,

orion take leave of that arrogant
posture, heard a most unreasonable

laughter, which you called mine,
pulling us down in fear beneath

the moon frayed at the edges of
a rotten, final phase, the sheer

fraudulence of constellations
revealed at last—nothing there

except solitary stars: one and
one and one and one and never a

series or a sum and only the one
device to grasp between us for

journeying among them: a rocketry
of old desires, strapped to the

momentum of bones in a dark place.

agate hunting at two harbors

your brother was an icicle,
your sister a small flame.
hung between the two of them
you kept your cradle turning and turning.

your father had hands like geodes
but your mother mined for gold, gold;
they were the rocky vacuum you turned in
when your siblings cancelled each other out.

and you: you wanted the solid touch:
lava, water, mica, bones: whispers

turning in the earth to say,
'feel *me*, feel *you*.'   today,

your children have hands like fire,
like ice.   their fingers drum
dim threats and promises along your bones,

and you yourself dream agate dreams,
stones with true pulses in them:

on a long beach of changeable rocks
you turn slowly, calling me
to come and see what you value.

first principle of aerodynamics

look, she said, at that tiny world
down there below: people, houses,
everything so far away and small.
in her flesh she proclaimed, we fly!
in my words i countered, can it be?

but the words came apart in the wind
and tangled themselves in our wings:

only meant to greet our flight,
they said goodbye to its possibility.

still clinging tight, we fell and fell.

conservation

a giant sea-bird founders on the muck
that coats my bones.
his feathers darken and wither,
and he threatens to go down.

i arrive in the nick of time,
spreading straw and hope on the surface,
bringing the necessary detergents
to cleanse his feathers.

but i can't reach him.
he's too far out on that white shelf.
half gone already,
he cranes his long neck about,
shrieking.

then he's out of sight.
nothing i can do will ever bring him back.
ever.
all is quiet on the cluttered surface.
i can see i've only added to the mess.

suddenly i'm carried away by a commotion in my bones.

the antepenultimate flying poem

of all diseases
that i know,
the softening
of bone's the
worst. but where
o where does all
that hardness go?

it flies, says
mother: all that
calcic white is
drifting up there
in our skies.

like chalk, she
says. or dreams?
i argue: taking
all those shapes,
that bony powder
still manages to
be no more than
what it seems.

it seems, she
says, to be
about to rain.
heaven's loss,
i mutter, and
not necessarily
our gain.

traveling man for whom there are no vacations

carrying his frail canoe
across the threshold like

a bride, he eased it down
into the dark ohio. i'll

go upstream, he said, and
paddled off like a hunted

desperado till none could
see him any more. what old

random meanderings did he
find then? what weedy bogs

or ragged shorelines that
refused to fit the contours

in his eye? what underground
stream that took him deep

and north at last to this:

round and round he goes,
counterclockwise, trying

to wear the lakeshore down
into circularity. soon now

he'll plant his paddle neck
deep in some murky slough,

lean back and let the lake
take its own curious shape

around the drifting canoe,
islands appear where they

do least good. meanwhile,
lakes breed like poems in

the marshes of his mind,
scraping their pike teeth

down among the lily stalks.

ceremony

the loon broke in
but no one was home
to his empty laugh

the maggots invited
the loon to remain

cleared the aisles
for our procession

eight kinds of moss
cushioned our knees

flies and mosquitoes
catechized us

blessed this feast
we entered upon and

sanctified the night:

we pissed in the rain

tired old birches
dropped in our path

deer pieces covered
the nakedest rocks

i read and i read—
all that i read was

my cock   it is dead
from the neck up

and the bones of pike
scrape for attention

then it was twilight
and now hours later
it is twilight still

Tuska 1972

daedalus en famille

we rose to triplets: not
all at once, mind you, but
close enough, close enough.

they dozed, we all drifted.
always that tendency to
drift.   ah, how i fought it!

stay in here by my wings,
i demanded, make use of my
slipstream, glide easily.

they were awake now.   i
continued their education:
remember, i told them,

only the constant breath
of millions below keeps
us aloft.   but i forgot

what a surprise such news
would be down there.   whole
populations gasped, skies

bowed inward underneath
us, i flapped and flapped
and yet the irrevocable

spin came on, the wind
screaming through fingers
that touched as we fell

and i said to her, look!
for far back up above us
the children looped and

climbed, each one soaring
in the dense atmosphere
of his own sudden being.

ii. the house of the would-be gardener

1

you can tell from the mail it's
almost spring.   seed catalogues
drive you right out of your mind.
you call up an old girlfriend,
thinking maybe things have changed.
while her phone rings you look out
the window and watch snow patches

melt before your very eyes.   then
she answers, with a breathless hello
as if she's come rushing from her
shower just to answer your call.
'hello,' she says, 'hello hello hello.'
your own throat goes dry, and your
voice cracks when you try to speak.

you look at the phone as if it were
a gleaming piece of black fruit
and the vine from which it hangs
had only begun to grow.   'who's there?'
it cries, then the wire comes after
you, winding its great loops around

your arms and legs.   'wrong number!'
you scream, writhing among its many
tendrils, but remembering, as it
tumbles you to the floor, the dream
in which you planted the seed.   'who's
there?'   it whispers, coyly, at the end.

2

every drawer is a seed chamber
and you go through all of them,
fingering the tarnished silver,

underwear, boxes of old checks.
in one of them you know the seed
of your death has been planted,

and perhaps is already sprouting
from among the rolled socks or
out of the pages of a photo album.

you have no intention of doing it
any harm. you're a sincere gardener
if an unlucky one, aligning the rows

ever so devoutly, though the rains
come always too early or too late.
but here at last is the ideal crop:

it grows through all seasons yet
requires no attention. and when it
bears the fruit is yours, all yours.

for now you just want one look at it.
you want to see its size and shape
and what it's doing there in the dark.

drawer after drawer you fling open,
looking in vain to see it stretching
its slender green neck up at you.

at last you give up and go outside.
standing on the porch before the dark
house, you turn and squint at the sun.

3

you are down in the basement trying
to make the bulbs do good things at
an early stage. above you, the house

exhales damp, elegant fumes which are
carried off by the north wind. 'dahlia,
dahlia,' you repeat, holding the cold

shape in your bare hands, but it just
lies there, and flecks of peat moss
hang in the air between the two of you.

at last the house shudders in the cold
and turns inward, spilling its moist
overheated odors into your once-dry

basement. gasping, you loosen your tie
and wade through puddles of the jungle
that descends upon you, not knowing

whether to cry out or fall to your knees
and drink. suddenly you feel the firm
pulse of the root beating in your hands.

4

you run about flinging open all the doors
you can find and sowing yourself wildly

into room after room after room until
they all begin to open to one another

and the whole house opens to the outside.
now you look for any last, single barrier:

the broom closet, the basement door. you
swing each wide, seeking the critical mass.

finally the whole house begins to tremble.
you stand in the center of kitchens and baths,

watching chimney bricks crumble, china tip
off shelves, beds stagger across the floor.

but soon everything settles back down. only
the wind bangs things about now. the rain

whips through open doorways, and you tiptoe
carefully about, closing everything up,

very gently. then you tamp it down firmly
and go to bed, your work done for the moment.

Tuska 1972

5

you stand at the beginning of the field
and wait for something to happen.
rain clouds come up out of the west

with nothing to say to you. the ground
trembles slightly beneath your feet.
giant weeds fan out their leaves

one by one at the edge of the woods
and you go off in the other direction,

toward the house, finding your shoes
suddenly full of earth and pebbles.

the sun goes down, down, down, down . . .

then when it's dark the answers to all
the questions arise from the underbrush
and take flight. from behind locked doors

you listen all night while their
dripping beaks go over, moving north.

in the morning the fields are bare.
rabbits emerge from their warrens
to tend their wounded and dying.

6

under a single light you consider
the condition of your grapes. the radio

says to you, 'new moon wine tastes sour,
sour,' you live in an almanac

of caution, holding the fruit in your hands
just so. then the time comes to see

how things are arranged. you open the door.
over your head the moon goes up and down,

up and down, full to bursting.
at long last you cease looking for precedents

in your morality of tides and begin
to move with it, up and down, up and down,

all night long, squeezing your hands
and letting the thick, sweet juice run out.

7

you play the human scarecrow
at the top of the hill,
but water doesn't fear you.
the flood comes up and up and up,
crossing all your fences,
and its small waves dance
down the furrows toward you.

you are guarding the last seed
in the world, and you stand on it
only to protect it. 'go away,'
you cry to the dark waters,
'destroyer, provocateur, extremist!'

when at last the flood recedes,
it leaves seeds scattered
all over the hillside behind it.
you stand dry and embarrassed
at its departure, then you
follow it downhill toward home.
before you get halfway there
the whole hill begins to sprout.

8

all the preparations that a man can possibly make
you have made. the sun hangs upon its proper hook;
crows and squirrels have taken your warnings to heart;
weeds, weeds: they wouldn't dare.

now you look at your hands, you look at the earth
ground into them, and wonder, was it enough?
what will the clouds say?
the pebbles?
the slope of the hill?
night?

you have done what you could.
it was, in short, no relief.   none the less,
you synchronize your watch with the corn and the beans,
plant yourself in your favorite chair,
and close your eyes to soften the blow.

9

it is night. you make a vow to stop
opening and closing doors.
it's time to leave things the way they are.
the mold that creeps in under the snow
and does irrevocable damage to the grass
is nothing to you. you are not
grass. if you were . . .

but you are not. not grass. the mold
feeds upon you all the same.
it is compared to a grey spider
and its legs walk out in all directions
from a beginning no one's ever seen.
you whisper in the face of the mirror,
'love that spider, you,'

and then the snow is all gone,
and the doors are the way you left them,
open to what the plants are doing
in the dark, and you can hear the land
tilting to let the fertilizer run
downhill in your direction,
and finally the house itself lights up,
and everything out there turns toward it.

10

you look closely at your features
in last summer's color photograph,
taken when the corn was hip-high and
you dared to stand in the midst of it.

you can see care all over your face.
anyone can see it: how it's glossy
and how, since the season permitted,
you've lavished it all around you.

that must have been almost labor day.
the corn never got much higher, and
then you stepped out of the garden
and the photograph was all over.

but upstairs in a drawer you still
have the negative. and it shows how,
all through september, that garden
tended you, and licked its chops.

11

you feel that dreams are your right
as well as any other man's,
especially this early in the season,
and so you start one from seed,

but soon it blossoms into a giant
beanstalk and you have to dream
an axe to chop it down with
before things get too difficult.

then you start dreaming an eggplant
as big and purple as the world,
but when you sit back to admire it
you recall how long it takes to grow

at this northern latitude, and how
your children hate it, one and all.
what's left? you begin to wonder,
dismissing all the ordinary vegetables

as ordinary. just then a strange stalk
erupts, a thing you've never seen
before. but you know right off it's
kohlrabi, and wonder how it'll taste.

12

the president has decreed
that there are some places
in the world where nothing
is ever to grow again.
you see it in the paper.
not anything, it says, *ever.*
by the time you're done reading
about it, the president has
long since gone off to bed.

but you worry at those words,
say them aloud in front of
your mirror, and discover,
in the dark and weedy shapes
that sprout from your mouth,
that their roots are not
in ancient languages but in
your own throat and lungs:

and you vow to uproot them,
bloody as it may be. now,
in the dark, with no one
watching. you bend your head
over the toilet bowl, grab
the thorny stalk with both
hands, tug, and hear your
president clutch at his chest
and cry out in his sleep.

13

on a night of ultimate despair
you long for the turnip so perverse
that in july it begins to become an onion.

you go out in the dark with a flashlight
and start grubbing in the earth for it.
you only want to uncover it for a moment,

curse it, wish it luck, tamp the earth
down hard over it
and hurry inside with dirty hands

to fondle the roots, the stems, the fruit,
the shapes, the tastes of your own perversity.

14

you project a meal far in the future,
served by unknown hands, where
you arrive in style with the whole family,
whispering to the children, 'manners, manners.'

but all you get are cold, soggy vegetables:
carrots with no sign of life left in them,
peas in a state of advanced decomposition,
motionless asparagus.

you wince and start to push your chair back
but the children cry out loudly at you,
'manners, manners!'
and so you follow their heady example
and begin to eat.

at the end, full and heavy, you see
a grey slime left on every plate.
you identify it as the death
of all those vegetables, and dream
you have raised the wheat
to make the bread
to sop it up with:

one piece of bread you give to each one
who has shared in the planting, the weeding.
what you have raised you take inside you,
wiping and wiping till the plate is clean.
only then are you free to leave the table.

15

you are at the borders of a foreign country
with a fence instead of a passport in your hands.
the natives look down and refuse to acknowledge you.
nothing you can say will make them let you in.

indifferent to who has planted them there,
they leave you to be inspector of your own customs.
can you vouch for yourself that you're no smuggler?
what is it you really have to declare?

'what a day!' you cry. you ram the fence
into the baked earth, but it falls on its side at once.
obviously you didn't mean it. a cheer arises

from behind you. another tourist like yourself?
a travelling businesswoman? an international spy?
she carries neither papers nor luggage

but praises the rate of exchange and takes your hand
to lead you across your own fallen fence. in the center
you both fall down among the stalks, the dirt, the weeds,
and begin to nibble on whatever comes to hand.

16

the message that arrives in a dry spring
offers you a sympathy to which you are
less than sympathetic. 'who needs rain?'

you demand of the messenger. you resent
a weather not wholly yours. a dust storm
begins to swirl up from deep inside you.

'i'm only a messenger,' the messenger says.
but already your resentment has taken root
and begun to compete with the tomato plants

for the nutrients in the soil. the day
darkens: rabbits scurry for their burrows;
birds fall silent; you remember messengers

in stories bearing the pain of bad news.
but this one believes. you see it in how
she dances her dance of understanding,

in the way she treats the storm you storm
as an act of real weather—taking shelter
under her own bare arms and then applauding

when the sky clears. and you applaud too:
you've weathered three sorts of weather now,
and when she forms herself into the sign

for 'rain' the ground is immediately moist,
weeds of the worst sort come loose at once,
you know just what you need and find your

self in the act of carrying messages to her

17

you still spade the ground with your old ineptitude,
slaughtering worms, hacking roots to bits.
you refuse to tell the great clumps of earth
what you expect of them, but you expect it all the same.

then you hurl seed after seed after seed down into it:
too close together, too far apart, ignoring
kinds, depths, rows, mounds, sunshine and shade,
seasons of temperance. stamping and stamping you
pack it all down hard underneath you with both feet.

only when it's all over do you read the directions.
they say, 'what kind of gardener are you, anyway?'
you wonder yourself: is there anything else to plant?

so you go back into the house and set about once more
flinging open doors, rummaging through cabinets.
at last you come upon your own package of bones.
you read what it says there—'late hybrid.
terribly susceptible to frost. plant deep, deep.'—
and then you go out and begin to dig all over again.